Releasing the Universe Within

LIFTING AWARENESS
INTO THE REALM OF *I AM*

Other Books by Paul F. Gorman

The Great Need

I Am (A Meditation)

I Am Now (A Meditation)

One

The Miracle Self

The Giving Self

Healing of The Body

The Way of Awakening

Satisfied With God Alone

Bringing Forth The Presence of God

Anyone Can Demonstrate Infinity

The Impersonal Self

The Inner Sanctuary

The Seven Spiritual Steps To Solving Any Problem

Opening The Windows of Heaven

Only God Is

The Fully Manifest Presence

That Which You Seek

Many free writings at www.miracleself.com

Releasing
the
Universe
Within

LIFTING AWARENESS
INTO THE REALM OF *I AM*

PAUL F. GORMAN

VINE
PRESS

NAPA
CALIFORNIA

Releasing the Universe Within: Lifting Awareness into the Realm of I AM

Copyright © 2018 by Paul F. Gorman

FIRST EDITION

ISBN-13: 978-0-9990218-6-6
ISBN-10: ISBN-10: 0-9990218-6-9

Published by Vine Press, Napa, California

www.miracleself.com

Available from Amazon.com and other online
nd traditional book stores worldwide

"My food is to do the will of him that sent me,
and to finish his work." John 4:34

Think of yourself as a diner as you read this book.
The "food" herein has been presented for you
exactly as a Master Chef would plate his or her food
— with ample space for seeing and appreciating
each bite, with space for savoring and lingering,
with a presentation that is worthy of the value of
the food, worthy of the beauty and love that it is.

M.L., Editor

Rise in conscious awareness — this is the entire secret.

As conscious awareness rises, detaching from and
leaving behind belief, ever greater degrees of heaven
become visible through the unconditioned mind.

"As in heaven so in earth."

The earth and all its people, things and conditions
are witnessed unconditioned, whole and harmonious,
love and union of all emerging through the dissolving
fog of false sense.

Indeed, "As in heaven so in earth" emerges as the one
reality. The bondage of false, material sense is dispelled,
and the unconditioned reality of man, earth and universe
is experienced harmonious, peaceful and free, in love.

Paul F. Gorman

CONTENTS

CONTENTS

CONTENTS

PREFACE

A need remains among spiritual students who have spent years studying and meditating yet still find themselves struggling with ill-health, lack, limitation, disharmony or decrepitude.

Freedom in spirit on earth comes not only by knowing that God is all but by knowing why *appearance* consists of both good and bad. The truth of life must be known, but the reason for apparent untruth must also be known. "Know the truth, and the truth will make you free."

Once untruth is known for what it is (believed reality with no substance, law or activity of its own to uphold it in one's experience) it can be ignored while the fullness of God is witnessed within. *Then* truth shines "through" the window of unconditioned mind to reveal the harmony of body, thing and condition.

In this book of seventy-one inspired lessons we are given profoundly clear and practical answers and are guided in the practice of the presence of God — within *and without* — which releases the universe of Good as tangible everyday experience.

As individual awareness is filled with truth, the light of God realization shines within and without, revealing a world of good without opposite where, to material sense, bad appeared to battle with good.

Illumined awareness is the secret of "earth as it is in heaven." As our conscious awareness lifts into the realm of God we are filled with the light of clear seeing. This illumined vision is what "human" sense describes as the miracle of healing, abundance, love, harmony and peace. These are not miracles in themselves but that of illumined seeing. "Whereas I was blind, now I see."

As you journey into the universe within give yourself the gift of at least one significant period of silence each day, simply letting *I be I as I* as *I is* as you. In this silence of personal self the light of *I Am* shines brightly and the goodness of God is tangibly witnessed.

LESSON
ONE

The universe of apparent material form is, in reality, the one universe of consciousness (God, spirit and truth, infinity, omnipresence).

Because the only consciousness in your universe is *you*, and the only consciousness in mine is *me* (the kingdom of God is within you; the whole of God exists in and as you), your whole universe is your consciousness, and my whole universe is my consciousness.

Not a single person, thing, place, condition, activity or amount in your universe is outside of, separate from or different from *you* (the consciousness you are).

All is, and exists within you. You are the god (the entirety) of your universe.

We have heard this truth a thousand times, but we have not taken it literally. In order to experience the true, harmonious universe, we must now take it literally.

Consciously realize and take literally: everything I experience this day is my sense of what he, she or it truly is (God).

Therefore, ask, What am *I being* as this person, thing or condition in my experience today?

Be assured that whatever you accept as being real in your universe, whatever you react to in your universe, whatever you are afraid of and protect yourself from in your universe, whatever you accept as lacking or limited or disharmonious in your universe *is you accepting belief, you accepting concepts of reality, you accepting pairs of opposites* instead of oneness, instead of having God as *literal* and *practical* all.

I am with you — *I* am being your truth — 24 hours a day. Rest, dear friends; *rest,* and *let* your *I am* light shine as you and for you.

LESSON
TWO

What I am accepting in belief is what I am *being* in this minute's experience.

All is, and exists within you. You are the god (the entirety) of your universe.

Continuously ask, What am *I being* as person, thing, place, amount and condition in this minute's (this now's) experience?

What am *I being* as I, mind, body and earth this minute, this now?

Let us deeply understand what we heard in Lesson One: Whatever we accept as being real in our universe (an entity in and of its own self), whatever we react to, bad or good, in our universe, whatever we are afraid of and protect ourselves from in our universe, whatever we accept as lacking, limited, disharmonious, burdening in our universe *is our accepting belief, accepting concepts of reality, accepting the manifest experience itself as a reality; is we ourselves being hoodwinked by belief and its false imagery; is we ourselves accepting and operating within pairs of opposites* instead of oneness, instead of having God as literal and practical all of all.

God, good, is all. There is no other; there is no other form — no other person, thing or condition.

My kingdom is the living consciousness of this one and only reality.

Live consciously *in* God as all of all.

Live consciously *with* God as all of all.

Live consciously *as* God as all of all.

Live consciously as "the one son of God," for there are not many sons – just one, that one being the *I* you are, the *I* I am, and the *I* that is all in our individual experience of My kingdom.

LESSON
THREE

Only God is, and God is silence; therefore only silence is.

To have the tangible experience of God, have the tangible experience of silence.

There is no other way to experience God (good) because there is no other God.

Lift yourself into silence in which and as which nothing of pairs of opposites exists in you, and no reaction to opposites exists in you; in which and as which only God exists as literal, palpable, visible formation:

God inside you, God outside you.

Silent inner, silent outer.

No bad, no good; no pairs, no opposites.

No judgment, no idea, no concept; no reaction, no effort.

Just God, just *is*, just *silence*, just *I* living *I am*.

LESSON
FOUR

No one can give you that which you yourself do not have.

The world cannot give you that which you yourself do not have.

Person, thing, condition, amount, activity or place cannot give you as itself that which you do not have as it.

I is what you are, and *I am* is what you have.

Be *I* and give *I am* to all-of-all mind, body and world.

Realize, I can receive only that which *I have* and *am being* as the all-of-all of my world.

There is no one else, nothing else, to receive it from.

LESSON
FIVE

When we have as much God in (as) the outer as we do the inner, God (good) is as real and palpable to our outer sense as to our inner.

But if we have God inside and a human outside; God inside and a thing, condition, amount or place outside; infinity and omnipresence inside but finiteness and objective presence outside; the nameless inside but the named outside, then we have a divided consciousness and in that division, that separateness, God is hidden from sense.

In other words, if we are attempting to bring health, wealth, love, harmony or peace to that which we believe needs it, we fail. When we know all *as being* health, wealth, love, harmony and peace (the presence of God, good) *despite every appearance to the contrary,* we quickly have these filling our outer experience.

The inner and outer can only give us what we *have.*

This is why we watch so many students experiencing wonderful, peace-filled (even ecstatic) meditations "inside," yet experiencing as much good v. bad as any human "outside." This is why those seekers cannot heal; and it is why *we* cannot until we lift into the consciousness of oneness, the consciousness that *is* My Universe.

Meditate deeply with this, and with the following Scriptures:

> For whosoever hath, to him shall be given, and he shall have more abundance: but whosoever hath not, from him shall be taken away even that he hath. Matthew 13:12

> Yeshua said to them, When you make the two into one, and when you make the inner like the outer and the outer like the inner and the upper

like the lower, and when you make male and
female into a single one, so that the male will not
be male nor the female be female . . . then you
will enter the kingdom; Know what is in front of
your face and what is hidden from you will be
disclosed. There is nothing hidden that will not
be revealed. *Gospel of Thomas*, Sayings 22; 5

LESSON
SIX

Think deeply on
   Meditate deeply upon
      Be the deep silence of

I am

(not personal I am)

LESSON
SEVEN

I am is silence.

    Nothing but *utter receptive silence* is *I am* experienced. Hear it with hearing ears; see it with seeing eyes.

    I am is silence. Nothing but *utter receptive silence*
        is *I am* experienced.

    Now decide what you will do about the sound of heaven you are hearing and the light of heaven you are seeing.

    "Choose you this day whom ye will serve . . . As for me and my house, we will serve the Lord [I am]." Joshua 24:15

LESSON
EIGHT

God (*I am*) is *silence.*

Thinking is not *I am,* therefore is not (and cannot be) God, good, evidenced.

Doing is not *I am,* therefore is not (and cannot be) God, good, evidenced.

Only *silence is;* only *silence* evidences itself; only *silence* sees itself.

Therefore, only silence is God, good, evidenced.

Do you hear, do you see? *I am* is silence; therefore nothing but utter *receptive silence* is *I am (good) experienced.*

LESSON
NINE

God — silence — is instantaneity.

God — silence — *is*.

Taking thought for our lives removes us from silence, therefore from instantaneity.

Belief, concept, idea are "noisy self" not silence, therefore remove us from instantaneity.

Effort, activity, power, might are "noisy self" not silence, therefore remove us from instantaneity.

In and as and "through" silence, all already (instantly) is.

LESSON
TEN

"Awake, O sleeper and rise from the dead, and Christ shall give you light [senses shall be illumined to reveal self-completeness in every way, form and condition, limitless and free to be the fullness of spiritual being on earth]."
Ephesians 5:14 (Lamsa translation)

Nothing of good — nothing, nothing, *nothing* of utter oneness, completeness and fulfillment of being — is absent or separate from immediate experience.

Why? *I am* is oneness (omnipresence), not twoness, not separateness, not difference, not multiplicity, not pairs of opposites, not variability, not uncertainty, not condition.

I am that, not I *can be* or *will be* when I sufficiently rise in spiritual awareness; *I am* . . . *I am* . . . *I am* . . . because only God is. Only My Universe exists; there is no other (only in false sense do we believe there is another, then act out of the belief in otherness).

The realization of *I am is* the spiritual awareness that reveals the fulfillment of being.

Every minute we spend *attempting to become I am* is another minute we keep ourselves separated in sense from our wholeness and fulfillment.

Every minute we devote to *realizing I am* is another minute devoted to the single most powerful and effective awareness in heaven and earth: the infinity and eternal oneness (self-completeness) of being.

LESSON
ELEVEN

My Kingdom is the only kingdom.

Spiritual mind is the only mind and is forever fully aware of — and being — its self-complete self (infinite and omnipresent fulfillment of being).

But remember, "The carnal mind is enmity against God: for it is not subject to the law of God, because it cannot be." Romans 8:7 (Lamsa)

Never forget this. If we continue in a dream state believing that person, thing or condition is in *any way* separate, different or less than the full presence and form of God — the literal, real and practical presence of God, oneness, good ("If you see me, you see the Father who sent me") — then we are not subject to the law of God (the visible, palpable, literal and practical truth), because we cannot be.

It is like realizing that a belief in 4 x 4 being 8 is not subject to the law of math because it cannot be.

Hear it . . . hear it. If we believe that any person, thing, condition, circumstance, amount, activity or place is anything *but the very full presence and form of God,* then God (true good) is entirely unavailable to our experience.

No matter how lovingly and devotedly we attempt to "bring God to carnal (separated, divided) sense," we fail for the single reason that a belief in twoness (carnal mind; inner versus outer; spiritual versus human, physical, material, earthly) "is not subject to the law of God, because it cannot be."

I am . . . I am . . . I am.

Meditate upon this one, already self-fulfilled truth for hours and hours.

A consistent *I am* meditation will do more for you than a thousand others.

LESSON
TWELVE

My universe (the infinite, omnipresent consciousness that is spirit and truth) is the only universe.

My being is the only being.

My mind, and the infinity it is, has and is aware of, is the only mind.

My body, and all that *My* body is, is the only body.

My thing, condition, amount, activity and place are the only thing, condition, amount, activity and place.

The belief in *anything whatsoever* being different or less than the fullness of God is what Saint Paul has called "enmity against God." Really, it is enmity against ourselves and our experience of wholeness and harmony, for it is only we who suffer by our mistaken awareness.

Certainly, God does not suffer! In fact, God knows nothing about our erring, our belief and the unwittingly needless suffering it brings about.

The moment we believe God is even slightly absent in and as the actual presence and form of person, thing and condition; the moment we attempt to get God to show us wholeness and harmony, to heal, love, prosper or pacify that which we believe needs it, we have instantly separated our sense from God, and in so doing have violated the law, the presence and principle of wholeness, of omnipresence, of "Ye are ever with me, and all that I have is yours."

Remember — 1000 times a day — "The carnal mind is enmity against God: for it is not subject to the law of God, because it cannot be." Romans 8:7 (Lamsa)

Then lift into and maintain a living awareness of

I am . . . I am . . . I already am.

As we heard in Lesson Eleven, meditate upon this one already self-fulfilled and self-sustained truth for hours upon hours.

And trust it when we are told: *a consistent I am meditation will do more for you (will reveal more God, good, in your life) than a thousand others.*

LESSON
THIRTEEN

My existence is the *only,* and *I am spirit and truth,* not matter and untruth or nonfulfillment.

I cannot be named; *I* am non-definable; *I* am non-detectable to material sense and to divided consciousness (God within "and" something less than or different from God without); yet *I* am the one actual, palpable, practical, visible reality fully palpable and visible as and to My Self.

The apparent, in itself, is not *I*. Only *I* itself is *I*.

If we believe and make effort for anything apparent we are not in *I*-consciousness and therefore, cannot experience *I* as the apparent.

When we stay in *I*-consciousness as and for the glory of *I* alone, we witness *I* as the glory of the apparent.

"I must be about my Father's business," not the business of the apparent.

Then, and then only, am I in truth; and then, and then only, do I *have* truth at hand as my ever-present, real and practical experience.

LESSON
FOURTEEN

"The law is not of faith: but, the man that doeth them shall
live in them." Galations 3:12

I am is itself the law made evident.

As we *be omnipresent I am,* we are subject to the law of
God, because we can be [we have made ourselves "available"
to the law of God by *being it*].

LESSON
FIFTEEN

"The law is not of faith: but, the man that doeth them shall live in them." Galations 3:12

Law — principle — is infinite, omnipresent, omnipotent and omniscient (the intelligence, wisdom, power, form, activity and visibility of *itself alone*).

Its universe is *full of itself* alone. The fullness of its oneness exists "inside itself and outside itself," *as all there is.*

It is not influenced by any person, thing or condition because there is no "other or different" person, thing or condition in its universe.

Only *it itself* exists *as* and *throughout* its universe, *being all its universe constitutes* (No matter how all may appear to sense as person, thing or condition. "Judge not by the appearance".).

"I am the Lord, and besides me there is none else." I am the law (the principle), and besides me there is none else.

It is this absolute, no-exceptions *oneness* "inside you and outside you" that evidences oneness (health, wealth, love, harmony, peace) as form.

In other words, law (principle) experiences itself "inside and outside" *as it is being nothing but itself,* as it considers nothing but itself, as its purpose consists of nothing but self-purpose (law, principle, truth, God purpose).

"I must be about the Father's business." I must be about the business (consistently and with utter discipline of sense) of knowing that *all is I am.*

The business of being "I am" within, yet believing that "he, she and it" without are *not I am,* or are potentially I am, or "in truth" are I am, is nothing but belief's, the devil's, business (read the "three temptations of Christ" Matthew 4:1-11).

I am with you; *I am* as you; *I am* eternally one with and as you.

You are myself, *I am* yourself — one glorious, evident, fulfilled, experientially purposeful, free and joyous self.

LESSON
SIXTEEN

"The law is not of faith: but, the man that doeth them shall live in them." Galations 3:12

Law (principle) is evident as and to itself alone.

Once we know that all is (already) *I am,* and therefore no longer "deny God" by believing that any person, thing or condition is less than or different from God; when we continually resist the temptation to do anything to make what we believe is not God into God (to attempt to heal, prosper, pacify or harmonize), and get on with the Father's business of knowing, being and giving God alone, *then we are those who are "doing the law" and living in it (evidencing it).*

The moment we have person, thing or condition to which we are attempting to *apply* the law, we have taken ourselves right out of the law, and we fail.

God is evident to *itself alone* (because there is none else to be evident as or to or for).

Only God is!

LESSON
SEVENTEEN

All is God, one, *I am.* There is nothing in or about the entirety of existence but *I am.*

It does not matter how we define a person, a thing, a circumstance, a place, a condition. "Judge not by the appearance." *All* is God; all is *I am.*

"*I am* the first [the essence, the alpha, the within-ness, the spirit, the substantial], and *I am* the last [the form, the experience, the omega, the objective sense]; and beside me there is no God [no existence whatsoever]." Isaiah 44:6

The same truth is in the words of the Master: "The kingdom of heaven is inside you and it is outside you."

LESSON
EIGHTEEN

All is God, *I am.*

The 7.5 billion people on earth today are God *being* what we experience as 7.5 billion individual expressions of the one God, the one presence, the one *I am.*

What is the nature of God, truth? "It is the Father's good pleasure to give you the kingdom."

As we consciously realize that all beings are *I am*, and stop believing them to be human, we cannot help but pour everything that God is and has out to them and for them, and they cannot help but be God for us, pouring all that God is and has out to us and for us.

Imagine, when you know this truth and experience even a few people in your day, how much God (good) you are given.

The whole of infinity is present, visible and tangible, and pouring itself out to you as and from every person in your day, *when you truly know them as I am,* and nothing "else."

LESSON NINETEEN

"I am in this world" (John 9:39); "[but] I am not of the world." (John 17:14)

We hear in *The Great Need*

> At our current level of "human" awareness —
> "one of the many mansions in my Father's house"
> — mind is objective. Hence we have the
> experience of objectively formed life — time and
> space; cause and effect; the five senses of hearing,
> seeing tasting, touching, smelling. Because the
> mind is objective, our thoughts are objective. But
> realize, objective awareness and thought are
> simply our *sense* of oneness, experienced at and as
> our current level of awareness, or mind (which is
> objective).

I *sense* objectively but I am not *of* objectivity.

LESSON
TWENTY

"As long as I am in the world, I am the light of the world." (John 9:5)

As long as *conscious I am* is present as you and as me, *I am* visible truth revealed in and as the world.

But *I am* has to be *consciously* experienced, *consciously felt* as the life and presence of God living us, being the entirety — the inner *and* outer — of existence.

In other words, only as "we" — personal selves — are absent, is God present; only as "we" have let go of and relinquished the personal sense of life with its universe of need and desire and yielded to God, letting God live its own existence as us, is the objective sense (the world) illumined as the light (health, wealth, harmony and peace) it is; is earth revealed "as it is in heaven [as it is in truth]".

Meditate with this deeply, continually.

"As long as *I am* in the world,
I am the light of the world."

LESSON
TWENTY-ONE

"I pray not that thou should take them out of the world, but that thou should keep them from the evil." John 17:15

Living the illumined life of spirit does not take us out of the world but washes from our consciousness the belief in twoness, in separateness and difference from God.

All is God. As we know and live in oneness, the world and all it constitutes is witnessed as God (good), whole, harmonious and purposeful.

LESSON
TWENTY-TWO

"Sanctify them through thy truth: thy word is truth."
John 17:17

Let us take this deeply into awareness today, understanding that "through thy truth" means through the purity of God consciousness, of God being all-of-all, already fully present, manifested, demonstrated, visible, tangible and real to spiritual sense.

LESSON
TWENTY-THREE

"The kingdom of God is within you." Luke 17:21

This statement almost sounds like a cliche, we have heard it so many times. But do we *know* it? Do we *live* it? Do we *trust* it? Are we *being* it? Are we *being true oneness, true within-ness?*

Or do we still believe that the "inner" is different from the "outer"? Do we still seek our good, or some of it, or certain categories of it, from the outer, and by mental or material means, or both?

"Not by might, nor by power, but by my spirit, says the Lord of hosts [says the truth, the within-ness, of all that exists]." Zechariah 4:6

A miracle happens in individual experience when we meditate deeply and continuously on the truth that "The kingdom of God is within you." Can you imagine what happens when you truly know and live every minute of life as and by the kingdom within? Can you imagine the infinity of all good that is ever at hand; the unconditional love that all in your universe is and is witnessed as; the boundless good form, amount and activity ever available to you and for all in your consciousness; the omnipotent power of peace and harmony your very presence is to every person and condition in your world; the love, light, life, relationship, home, food, safety, protection, freedom, happiness your consciousness is *as* and *for* all people, all conditions, all places, all amount, all things?

Meditate on these things, in the realization that the entirety of existence, the kingdom of all that is (God, good) is within you, *is your consciousness,* and exists in full glory, fully manifested and demonstrated, fully visible at every point of itself at the same time.

Most importantly, remember that God (the truth of all that is) is spirit, not matter — not human, mental, physical, material.

"The kingdom of God is not meat and drink; but righteousness, and peace, and joy in the Holy Ghost [the spirit or consciousness of being]." Romans 14:17

I am with you in the secret place of the kingdom within. Together, in the consciousness and living of this realization, we are one; and as one, a mighty presence and power of light throughout and for the world.

LESSON
TWENTY-FOUR

The kingdom of God is within you." Luke 17:21

Not one aspect or form of good can come into your experience from outside of you; all good "comes from" within, and is beheld objectively as what is called "outer" or "worldly" good.

To believe that any good exists "out there," and to then seek and expect or hope for that good to "come" is as ludicrous in truth as it is to expect any scene of a movie to appear on the screen without first flowing forth from the projector in a cinema.

Meditate deeply on the truth that "the kingdom of God [literally all-of-all] is within you".

Then watch this realization change how you study, your meditations, your periods of silence, your thoughts and your actions.

LESSON
TWENTY-FIVE

"The kingdom of God is within you." Luke 17:21

The entirety of existence is within you.

Just as all thought exists within you and flows "from you into and as the world," so all people, things, conditions, places, amounts and activities exist within you and flow from you "into the world" (flow *as* the substance and form that constitute what we call our "world and universe."

All, all, *all* exists within you.

There is no way to experience any of God, good, without giving it, expressing it, pouring it out, contributing, sharing, serving — just as there is no way for a single frame of the movie to appear on the cinema screen without the projector giving it to the screen.

LESSON
TWENTY-SIX

"The kingdom of God is within you." Luke 17:21

We have heard this truth a thousand times; now we must take it one hundred percent literally, and *live it*.

All, all, *all* exists within.

Absolutely every person, thing, place, amount and condition exists within, and is witnessed "without" only because within-ness is "also," and "fills," the "outer" (objective) experience.

Withinness is the infinite omnipresence that *is* the one and only existence, the all-of-all (that which God is), experienced objectively as what we name "our world; person, thing, place, condition, activity, amount; the five senses; time and space, cause and effect; absolutely everything we name."

Simply stated, all that constitutes the universe is the infinite omnipresent within-ness beheld (experienced) objectively.

Observe a leaf, hear a bird's song, taste a serving of food, hold a flower, smell her fragrance, think a thought, sense self, *feel* life — all of this is your beholding within-ness objectively.

Just as we cannot experience a thought except by bringing it forth (giving it) from within, so we cannot experience truthful person, thing, amount, activity, place or condition without bringing it forth (giving it) from within.

Self is proactive ("It is the Father's good pleasure to give you the kingdom"), so the "outer" experience is automatic; however, if we are unaware of the truth of all, we merrily — or bleakly — encounter the "outer" with little or no God dominion substantiating it.

"Know the truth, and the truth will make you free." When we "join" the "Father's good pleasure" in giving the truth to our objective experience, we discover and have our freedom in and of all the earth "as it is in heaven [as it is in within-ness]."

LESSON
TWENTY-SEVEN

God does not have time or space in it.

God does not have cause or effect in it.

And God is the infinitude, the all-of-all. Therefore, the universe (our objective sense/experience of existence) does not have time or space, cause or effect in it.

Therefore, God does not have person, thing or condition in it because all these, as we sense them to be (as separate, different entities unto themselves, existing in time, occupying space, the effect of a cause) are concepts only and not God itself.

God *is.*

Illumination is the realization and the living of *is* being the only existence, substance, form, place, amount, activity and visibility.

True prayer is resting, bathing, in and as *is*, knowing that in is we are and have all that God is and has.

True meditation is the meditation of *is*, of *I am* and *I have* all; that I am a god (Psalm 82:6; Isaiah 41:23; John 10:34), not a beggar; that *I am* the one real and practical truth presence, substance and supply of my universe, not a victim in and of an untruthful universe which, somehow, I will fix by gaining God's help.

True silence is the silence of *omnipresent is*, as which there is nothing to "do" other than rest and radiate as *is*.

The moment we pray, meditate or sit in silence *for* a person, thing, condition, place or amount to *become* harmonious and true, we are out of God consciousness (out of My Universe) and are left with no way in heaven or in earth to evidence the *is* of God as all.

Realize: God *is*, therefore all that my consciousness is and beholds is *is*.

Know this truth, rest in and as *is*, and be free; in being free, watch as your *is*-presence reveals the mighty works of God as all that earth *is*.

LESSON
TWENTY-EIGHT

God does not have time or space in it; and because God is infinite-all, *nothing of existence including our objective sense of it* ("this world") has time or space in it.

Yes, time and space *appear* to exist; time and space are an aspect of our current three-dimensional *sense of that* which is, in actuality, here and now — as the only *true*, practical, invariable and reliable experience — 100 percent God, one, is-ness, now-ness, instantaneity . . . pure *is*.

Transcend the belief in time and space. Leave them behind just as you left your childhood home behind.

Lift into God sense — *is* — and live *there*. Think *there*, live *there*, move *there*, have your being *there*; insist that every moment of your existence is awareness of (and activity "out from") *is*, devoid of time-and-space belief.

Gently and lovingly wash yourself clean of the belief of every person, thing and condition, every place, every amount, every activity (every "reality") you have accepted as existing in, being an experience of, and being subject to time, and occupying space somewhere in mind, body or universe.

Watch how quickly you experience the release from "this world" ties, struggles, lack and limitation, suffering and pain as you begin to live free of the belief in time and space; for *all* bondage, struggle, lack, limitation, suffering and pain — *all* untruth — exist in time and occupy space. None exists in God *(is)*.

Exist as *is*, and let *is* exist as you ("abide in me, and I abide in you"), and be free.

LESSON
TWENTY-NINE

Now let us realize the same non-truth about cause and effect as we are realizing about time and space.

God does not have cause or effect in it; and because God is infinite-all, *nothing of existence including our objective sense* ("this world") contains cause or effect.

Yes, cause and effect *appear to be* in sensory experience; cause and effect are an aspect of our current three-dimensional *sense of that* which is, in actuality, here and now (as the only *true,* practical, invariable and reliable experience) 100 percent God, one, is-ness, now-ness, instantaneity . . . pure *is.*

And let me add, that the *apparent existence* of time and space and cause and effect in sensory experience *are innocent and impotent* as long as (and from the moment) we retract *belief* in them.

Transcend the belief in cause and effect. Leave them behind just as you left your childhood home behind.

Lift into God sense — *is* — and live *there*. Think *there*, move *there*, have your being *there;* insist that every moment of your existence is awareness of and activity "out from" *is*, devoid of cause-and-effect belief.

I am, I observe, I operate in the world without attachment, without belief, without reaction to that which seems to be.

I know that appearance is innocent and impotent in itself. Time and space and cause and effect are only pictures of sense. They are not real in themselves. Because they are not real they have no power, no influence, no reaction or result in me.

Gently and lovingly wash yourself clean of the belief of every person, thing and condition, every place, every amount, every activity (every "reality") you have accepted as existing in, being an experience of, and being subject to cause, and being an effect of or in mind, body or universe.

Watch how quickly you experience the release from

"this world" ties, struggles, lack and limitation, suffering and pain as you begin to live free of the belief in cause and effect; for *all* bondage, struggle, lack, limitation, suffering and pain — *all* untruth — exist as so-called cause and its effect (in other words, as the pairs of opposites in a tug of war with each other). None exists in God *(is)*.

Exist as *is,* and let *is* exist as you ("abide in me, and I abide in you"), and be free.

LESSON
THIRTY

God has no time, no space, no cause, no effect in it.

In the silence of God consciousness — in the *deep silence of being* — you are instantly free of all people, things, conditions, circumstances, amounts and places, all pairs of opposites, that seem so real and often "stuck" to a time-and-space, cause-and-effect consciousness.

The *deep silence of being* (nothing less) that *is* God consciousness *is itself* existence of freedom from all material (including Mosaic, Hebraic) laws, principles, and commandments.

The instant we attain the deep silence of being, we are free. Nothing human, mental, physical or material applies to us; nor can it operate in our lives.

Our constant purpose, therefore, is to re-attain and then maintain the *conscious deep silence of being* — true oneness in and as God, true existence as the finished kingdom, as a god, giving and serving of our omnipresent infinity, and knowing that *as we do,* we witness the multiplication of all good and fulfilling form.

Think deeply about this truth continuously until all belief in time, space, cause, effect is washed out of you).

The fruitage of truth depends on your deep realization of the non-reality of time, space, cause and effect — even in objective (world) sense/experience.

(Refer to Lessons 28 and 29 for more detail.)

LESSON
THIRTY-ONE

Because God has no time, no space, no cause, no effect in it, when you are in God consciousness (in the silence of oneness, *feeling* the presence of truth permeating you; without taking thought for any person, thing or condition; simply and silently bathing in and as *is*) *you are instantly free of every condition and consequence of time and space, cause and effect.*

You are "whiter than snow" (Psalm 51:7); you have no human, physical or material past, present, or future. You are, this instant, and for as long as you maintain true God consciousness (or keep re-attaining it each hour), devoid of the belief in and attachment to time and space, cause and effect; you are all that God is and has.

Rest *there;* rest as a completely impersonal self *there;* rest as *is,* and simply *behold* the presence of God announcing itself and blossoming, filling your mind, body and world with its heavenly fragrance, color, form and activity.

Do you see why you only need *behold God in action* when you are empty of belief and attachment, and live as the *is* of the finished kingdom of you presenting its abundant and glorious fruits to you each hour?

LESSON
THIRTY-TWO

When you are empty of the belief in and attachment to time what consequence of time could you suffer?

When you are empty of the belief in and attachment to space what consequence of space could you suffer?

When you are empty of the belief in and attachment to cause what consequence of cause could you suffer?

When you are empty of the belief in and attachment to effect what consequence of effect could you suffer?

None.

Only God is.

LESSON
THIRTY-THREE

I am the only; and *I am* has nothing to do with degrees of awareness; *I am* and the *I am experience* are not dependent on or conditional to individual awareness.

I am is, period (just as the sun *is,* gravity *is,* math *is,* aerodynamics *is*).

Knowing *this* is the greatest key to awakening (and the instantaneous key when it is truly known).

Only God is. No matter what "degree" of spiritual awareness we believe we have attained, we are having and can *only* have God experience because there is nothing but God.

It is impossible to have a non-God experience when the entirety of existence is God.

The minute we truly know and live *this* we are free.

I am the only existence and all that constitutes existence (all person, mind, body, thing, condition, place, amount, activity; the all-of-all — no matter what we name it).

Therefore, *I am* is the only experience.

Stop believing anything "different." Know the truth and the truth frees you.

Then live the rested state of being — *is* beholding *is.*

Live the life of the beholder, abundantly and ceaselessly giving and serving of that which presents itself to you. Simply behold the wonder of the finished kingdom blossoming and presenting its divine treasures and purposes to you *as and for all,* everywhere you are, and then *give . . . express . . . pour out* all you are and have.

"Where the spirit of the Lord is, there is liberty."

Merriam-Webster defines "liberty" as: the state of being free from the control or power of another. Synonyms: independence, self-governance, sovereignty, emancipation, release.

LESSON
THIRTY-FOUR

We heard in Lesson Thirty-Three that

> *I am* the only; and *I am* has nothing to do with
> degrees of awareness; *I am* and the *I am experi-*
> *ence* are not dependent on or conditional to in-
> dividual awareness.

> *I am is,* period (just as the sun *is,* gravity *is,* math *is,*
> aerodynamics *is*).

> Knowing *this* is the greatest key to awakening
> (and the instantaneous key when it is truly
> known).

Only God is. No matter what "degree" of spiritual awareness we believe we have attained, we are having and can *only* have God experience because there is nothing but God.

It is impossible to have a non-God experience when the entirety of existence is God.

The minute we truly know and live *this* we are free.

Today, let us lift into more fully "knowing and living *this*"; and in doing so, experiencing greater degrees of freedom and of giving-ness in every category of life.

Think what it is like to truly know God:

To truly know that *God is the only.*
To truly know that God is the finished kingdom of *all* — "inside you and outside you" — therefore, that all *is*, *this instant and eternally* (unchanging and unchange*able*, the

same yesterday, today and forever) perfection, harmony, wisdom, fulfilled purpose (of being, mind, body, thing, condition, place, amount).

To truly know that God is the all-of-all, the all-in-all, the all-as-all, the all-for-all.

To truly know that there is nothing you or I or even the Master can or needs to do to make God (good) so; that God, good, *is.*

To truly know that all is *omniscience and the formation thereof* (there is no such thing as "unformed" omniscience) -- the all-knowing, all-wise, almighty good that God is as *all* that is inside you and *all,* that is outside you.

Pause here, and think deeply — ponder, meditate upon — what has been said.

Now, where does this leave a personal "you" or "me"?

Where does this leave your or my effort or responsibility for life?

Where does this leave your or my effort in so-called

health and healing?

Where does this leave your or my effort for or involvement in evidencing supply, in feeding the multiples, in pacifying the storms, in being the light of the world?

Constantly, consciously, actively defer and yield to God — to that which all *is.*

Constantly, consciously, silently and receptively be a window of and for that which all *is.*

Constantly, consciously, spaciously, peacefully, effortlessly, patiently, silently *behold* that which all *is,* presenting itself to you, as you, for all in the range of your consciousness.

In a nutshell: truly, deeply know that *only I am is;* constantly, selflessly defer and yield to *I am;* live every moment as a window of heaven, a beholder of the heavenly riches freely filling your mind, body and world; freely and fully give, serve, share, express, contribute all the fruits of the kingdom to and with all in your world just as God freely and fully "gives, serves, shares, expresses, contributes all the fruits of the kingdom to and with all that you are and have."

"Ye are gods".

LESSON
THIRTY-FIVE

Truly, deeply know that *God — spirit and truth — is the only.*

Constantly, and more and more literally and completely, defer and yield to God, to spirit and truth.

Realize, "Where the spirit of the Lord is, *there* is liberty."

Liberty — "the state of being free from the control or power of another." (Merriam-Webster)

Constantly deferring and yielding to God, to spirit and truth; living the one true life of a beholder of the presence of God, good; being the giver — the god — of the gifts of heaven to all in your world *is itself* "the state of being free from the control or power of another" — free of God-"and"; free of this world; free of good vs. bad humanity, mental mind, physicality, materiality; free of every pair of opposites.

Realize each synonym for liberty as defining a God state of being with no personal self blocking its experience: *God is* independence, *God is* governance, *God is* self-sovereignty, *God is* emancipation, *God is* release.

Where the personal self is absent, the spirit of the Lord is present.

There liberty is tangible, visible and practical.

(Refer to Lesson 34 for more contemplation.)

LESSON
THIRTY-SIX

With spiritual discernment, let us take this verse from Romans 1 deep into meditation today, followed by much silent receptivity.

"For the wrath of God is revealed from heaven against all ungodliness and unrighteousness of men ["against" all belief, all material consciousness, all belief in existence being separate and different from God] who hold the truth in unrighteousness; because that which may be known of God is manifest in them; for God hath showed it unto them [God or truth is the only entity, the only reality; therefore a consciousness that is out of tune with that which is must, by definition, experience discord, lack and limitation]."
Romans 1:18-19

I Am with you as the light of this truth within.

LESSON THIRTY-SEVEN

Nothing is hidden in the mind of God.

As and with spiritual consciousness all that God is and has becomes visible to sense.

"For the invisible things of him from the creation of the world are clearly seen, being understood by the things that are made, even his eternal power and Godhead; so that they are without excuse." Romans 1:20

LESSON
THIRTY-EIGHT

"Because that, when they knew God, they glorified him not as God, neither were thankful; but became vain in their imaginations, and their foolish heart was darkened. Professing themselves to be wise, they became fools, and changed the glory of the uncorruptible God into an image made like to corruptible man, and to birds, and four-footed beasts, and creeping things." Romans 1:21-23

"Glorifying him not as God," etc., refers to *belief.*

Belief is itself the pairs of opposites, the un-God-like experience of "human, mental, physical and material reality" and the reliance on these as if bad were an entity in itself to be rid of, and its opposite, good (that which we seek to replace or heal the bad) were better entity that we should gain or achieve.

Meditate with this scripture and sit silently and receptive with it to hear your own clarity, to let its truth and fruitage flow as your tangible good.

LESSON
THIRTY-NINE

I was reading the Lamsa translation of our scripture this morning, and I think it is very helpful. Here it is for your additional contemplation and silence time today and beyond:

> For they knew God and did not glorify him and give thanks to him as God, but became vain in their imaginations, and their hearts were darkened so that they could not understand. And while they thought within themselves that they were wise, they became fools, and they have changed the glory of the incorruptible God for an image made in the likeness of corruptible man, and in the likeness of birds and of four-footed beasts and of creeping things on the earth.
>
> Romans 1:21-23 (Lamsa translation)

LESSON
FORTY

"Wherefore God also gave them up to uncleanness through the lusts of their own hearts, to dishonor their own bodies between themselves: who changed the truth of God into a lie, and worshipped and served the creature more than the Creator, who is blessed for ever. Amen." Romans 1:24-25

Again, meditate deeply with this scripture to hear your own clarity; and sit in much silence with it to let its fruitage come forth in awareness.

LESSON
FORTY-ONE

God *is.* Nothing "we" do or fail to do affects the ever-present *is* of God, therefore the ever-present *is* of all-of-all.

However, (and this is the entire crux of un-God-like experience, no matter whether we describe it as being disease, injury, lack, limitation, homelessness, starvation, insecurity, danger, injustice or immorality), because God is *consciousness* we must live in *conscious awareness of the presence of God* being the absolute only, the absolute all-of-all, despite appearance.

If we do not, or are not yet able to for lack of practice or discipline or both, it is as if God deserts us, but it is we who have deserted God.

Then we find ourselves in the experience of Romans 1 (and of all of scripture that describes the "pairs-of-opposites" experience of unawareness of the presence of God).

It is our *conscious awareness* of the omnipresence of God, our *consciously* living and moving and having our being in and as God, our absolute reliance on and as God alone as our all-of-all in the most real and practical way that *evidences* God, good, without our taking thought or action *for* our lives or any aspect or form of them.

> Take no thought [or action] for your life. . . . Which of you by taking thought [or action] can add to your life one cubit? If ye then be not able to do that thing which is least, why take ye thought for the rest? Rather seek ye [the *consciousness* of] the kingdom of God; and all these things shall be added unto you. Fear not, little flock; for it is your Father's good pleasure to give you the kingdom. Luke 12:22; 25-26; 31-32

LESSON
FORTY-TWO

God is consciousness, and God is all; therefore consciousness is all. "All things were made by him; and without him was not any thing made that was made." John 1:3

All that *is* is consciousness, and exists "in" or "within" and as consciousness. And because God or consciousness is *one* — omnipresent, indivisible, forever self-whole, self-sustained — your and my individual consciousness (and that of every person) is the whole of consciousness (the whole of God).

We witness our consciousness objectively through the objective sense of mind and name it "this world" — "human, mental, physical, material; time, space, cause, effect" and so on.

"This world" is not a different world, a separate world, but is *the one existence*, which is God or consciousness simply *sensed* objectively.

Do you see, therefore, that the only thing that is ever sick, injured, lacking, limited or discordant is our *belief* about our sense of identity, and about that which we sense as other people, bodies, minds, things and conditions?

If (and immediately when) we *know* — truly, deeply, thoroughly *know* — that all is God, good; and that God — the "kingdom of heaven and of earth and all the host of them" — is finished, one, tangible, visible and omnipresent; and when we then literally "live and move and have our beings in God," our experience of self, mind and body, and of our world and all it constitutes becomes, to us, that which it is: God.

LESSON
FORTY-THREE

All is sensed as and from *within*. Nothing *in itself* (none of actual existence, no person, no entity) exists out there ("I of my own self can do nothing [because I of my own self am nothing; only God is]"); all is "in here" *sensed objectively as being "out there."*

We all know this! Yet how many times can we catch ourselves "spiritually working on" someone or some thing or condition out there in the belief that he, she or it needs God, needs truth, needs fulfillment; can be lifted, can be made whole, can be made harmonious and true?

Every minute of such effort is wasted in truth, for "I am; I already am; and I am the only."

"Take no thought for the things [appearances] of your life . . . rather seek the kingdom of God" — the kingdom, the presence of *I am*, of God as all, of the finished and perfect person, thing and condition of God, good — "and all these things [all truthful appearance] shall be added unto you [shall fill, shall be, your sense]."

LESSON
FORTY-FOUR

Everything witnessed in the presence of the Master was and is a picture of his consciousness, his within-ness. Nothing is "outer"; all is within, all is one, omnipresence; all is consciousness witnessed objectively.

Never did the Master apply "God consciousness" to an outer person, thing or condition that he believed was, at the moment, "not God" or "less than God" which, when God consciousness was "applied to" or "given to" would transform into a greater experience of God.

Every healing, every multiplied amount of food, every ounce of love and compassion, every clearly visible fruit and every experience of peace and harmony witnessed in his presence was, and is, the objective sense of his consciousness — the "outer" sense of his within-ness.

Let us meditate deeply on these truths, and let us work to be and to evidence the same, for "the works that I do shall ye do also; and greater works than these shall ye do."

LESSON
FORTY-FIVE

True oneness is its own evidence.

Deeply realize what we have heard in Miracle Self writings, that there is *no "evidence" of God in God consciousness.*

God *is,* which is far different from saying that God is *evident* (and believing that God can be).

For a state of good or truth to be "evident," it must also be able to be non-evident; for a state of good to be present, it must also be able to be absent.

In other words, the "evidence" of God as person, thing or condition is nothing more than the good side of the pairs of opposites.

There are no opposites in God; therefore good is not "available from" God. God is only evident as itself in which there is no evidence, but simply *is.*

God *is itself,* period.

Is *is itself,* period.

We must wash ourselves clean of the belief that we can "evidence God" where God, at this moment, seems to be absent.

We must be the god, the *is,* of existence *as which* nothing but true oneness is "happening."

LESSON
FORTY-SIX

Take this simple yet all-releasing truth deep into your being:

God *is,* and God is *all;* therefore all *is.*

If all *is,* there is no "evidence." *Is* is its own evidence.

In the omnipresence of *is* there is nothing "else"; therefore there is nothing else to evidence. *Is* is its own "evidence."

Hear it deeply:

Is is its own "evidence."

The minute we attempt to evidence nameable good, we are attempting to evidence something different from *is,* and we have failed before we start.

Never look "outside" of My Universe (outside of the universe of *is*) in an attempt to see how *is* will appear as nameable good.

Is "appears" only as itself because *is* is the only.

Only *is* is; *is* is its own evidence.

Once we have *is*, we have the whole universe of that which *is*, and never again find ourselves in lack or limitation of any good thing.

Know this truth; live the rested state of being in and as *is;* and behold God (*is*) visible and tangible everywhere about as the good, harmony and abundance of all.

LESSON
FORTY-SEVEN

Let us live with just this today:

God *is,* period. There is no "evidence" in God; there is only God in God.

God is its own "evidence."

Is is its own "evidence."

LESSON
FORTY-EIGHT

God *is;* and God is the *infinite,* the *only,* the *all-of-all.*

Nothing but God exists.

The fact that God is sensed objectively does not make an object out of God.

Only God is; in, out and as every point of the infinitude at the same time *only God is.*

It is because only God is that *only God sees God; only is sees is.*

We can state it in different ways:

Only a God state of being has and experiences a God state of form (person, thing and condition).

Only God consciousness has and experiences the God (true) state of form.

Be a god and you have God as all.

Be the "causal" presence — the God presence — of all, and you then have and see the "effect" of the cause you are being.

Be the God substance and form of all in your consciousness, and you then have and see God substance and form *as* all in your consciousness.

Be — see, hear, taste, touch, smell and think — nothing but God, and you then *have* nothing but God.

We must be god to have God.

We must be god to see God.

The Master stated it in many wondrous ways, including these:

> Abide in me, and I in you. As the branch cannot bear fruit of itself, except it abide in the vine; no more can ye, except ye abide in me. I am the vine, ye are the branches: He that abides in me, and I in him, the same brings forth much fruit: for without me ye can do nothing. John 15:4-5

"I am the light of the world: he that follows me shall not walk in darkness, but shall have the light of life." John 8:12

"Ye are the light of the world." Matthew 5:14

LESSON
FORTY-NINE

We must never separate God and form, God and experience, God and person, place, thing, amount or condition.

One is the only truth; therefore *our consciously being one* is the only experience-able God or truth or harmony.

When we are being consciously one as all, we see (we have) one as all.

We must be the *causal* presence, the god of our universe, the oneness of our universe.

Just as the subject in front of the mirror and the mirror image are one and cannot be separated, or believed to be separate, so God and form — God and the image and likeness — are one and cannot be separated, or believed to be separate.

One . . . one . . . one. That's it; there is nothing "else."

LESSON
FIFTY

God *is.* . . .

Nothing "else" is in the entirety of existence; therefore, *God is* its own evidence; *is* is its own evidence.

We have to *be* a god, *be is, be* the presence of God (not of our own selves, which is impossible; but by being constantly *consciously aware* of the presence of God "happening" within and as all), *be* the "cause" of God as all, *be* the consciousness of God being already and fully evident (there being no other possibility in the entirety of heaven and earth) to see and to have *is* (which is all that God is and has).

Watch, as we *rest in is,* rest in God-already-is, in God-is-the-only-is, therefore nothing to "do, heal, harmonize, prosper or pacify," how we then behold our minds, bodies and world filled with *that which we are being* — God, good.

The "cause" and the "effect" are one and inseparable.

Being the cause and the effect, one and inseparable, is the secret.

LESSON
FIFTY-ONE

"My kingdom is not of this world." John 18:36

Take *all* that constitutes "this world" out of your consciousness, out of your concern.

Do not take thought *for* anything of this world. If we take thought for person, thing or condition we are lost; we are out of My kingdom, out of truth, out of God consciousness and, therefore, cannot have any of God in practical experience.

Remember, we cannot have a partial amount of God. God is one, omnipresence, inseparable, indivisible. We're either one hundred percent in God or one hundred percent out. "No man can serve two masters: for either he will hate the one, and love the other; or else he will hold to the one, and despise the other. Ye cannot serve God and mammon [materialism, humanity, "this world"]." Matthew 6:24; Luke 16:13

We have to be "in" My kingdom to have it; we have to be in God consciousness to have God person, thing and condition; and when we are, we have its entirety. We *are being* and *have* what God *is* — infinity, omnipresence, instantaneity, now-ness, oneness. We have no one and nothing "else"; therefore, we are not serving any person, thing or condition of "otherness."

God consciousness is literal oneness; therefore we have to be *being* true oneness (oneness *as* everything everywhere) to *have* omnipresent health, wealth, love, harmony and peace.

This is why the Master said to the disciples, "I have food to eat that ye know not of." He was not only stating fact (truth), but also trying to share with the disciples the literal reality and practicality of God.

The disciples were still not in the "My kingdom" consciousness. They judged by human, material, structural sense as they observed their beloved Master teaching all morning without having eaten. Even after he gave them the secret — "I have food to eat that ye know not of" — they still did not understand. "The disciples said among themselves, What! did any man bring him something to eat?" John 4:33 (Lamsa)

Here's the account:

> In the mean while his disciples prayed him, saying, Master, eat. But he said unto them, I have meat ["food" in Lamsa's translation] to eat that ye know not of. Therefore said the disciples one to another, Hath any man brought him ought to eat? Jesus said unto them, My food is to do the will of him that sent me, and to finish his work. Say not ye, There are yet four months, and then comes harvest? Behold, I say unto you, Lift up your eyes, and look on the fields; for they are white already to harvest. John 4:31-35

Let us keep our eyes lifted up, and look upon all we sense; for all is already My kingdom, divine, whole and complete in every way.

LESSON
FIFTY-TWO

"I have food to eat that ye know not of."

God is one, omnipresence, omnipotence, omniscience.

I am is *the* one, *the* omnipresence, *the* omnipotence, *the* omniscience.

I am forever whole and complete; *I am* incapable of being separated, divided; being incomplete in any way or form; experiencing a lack or limitation of any of God *even in objective experience,* because *I am* is the one, the omnipresence, the omnipotence, the omniscience.

I am the food. Whether we are speaking of food for "just me," or for "all of us," or for the multitudes, makes no difference. There are no multitudes in God. God is one; God is one being, who is forever whole and complete, forever with food and with every other God state, quality and condition.

My kingdom is oneness; My kingdom is *the one* forever fulfilled.

There is no lack or limitation, there is no disease, there is no unhappiness, there is no yearning or need; there is just oneness, wholeness, fulfillment.

The Master was trying to show the disciples that there is no hungry person in God. The entire concept of hunger and of any other lack or limitation of omnipresent, visible, practical fulfillment is absurd in the "My kingdom" consciousness.

I am the food of the world; *I am* the light of the world; *I am* the love of the world; *I am* the life of the world, because the only true world is the "my kingdom" world.

LESSON
FIFTY-THREE

God is its own evidence. In other words, God consciousness *constitutes its own evidence* of good.

But the minute we separate "God" and "evidence" — the minute we attempt to "dispense" our God consciousness "to" a person, thing or condition we believe is not already the fullness of God ("in" the body, or "in" or "working for" our finances or our businesses, or "in" our families and "for" our loves ones, or "to" this or that neighborhood, country or world condition) — there is no way we can evidence the true good even though it is fully present and visible right where we believe it is not. We have blinded ourselves because of our separated sense.

Deeply realize that God *is* its own evidence.

God consciousness *constitutes* its own evidence "inside" and "outside."

LESSON
FIFTY-FOUR

My universe has nothing to do with a personal "you" or "me."

My universe, My kingdom, is God and God's, and is full of *God alone.*

We are each universal selves, not personal, local selves. I am not personal, local, human. *I am* is universal self.

Therefore, if we seek anything but God itself — as a god, for the God-itself experience, to God; if we seek anything but the *one universal good,* we fail. "Take no thought for yourself or the things of your life. . . . but seek the kingdom of God."

I am all; *I am* the only. "I am the Lord, and besides me there is none else." This does not refer to there being no other "God or Lord *within* existence" but to there being no other existence whatsoever.

The only self is God, universal, self. There is no "my personal self" in God. If we exist as a "my self" attempting to see and to have God for "our good" (even the "our good" of our friends, students and neighbors; and of the human multitudes of our world who are hungry, homeless, without love, poor and discouraged, threatened by disease, war or atrocity) we exist blind to that which is. It then seems as if the good of truth evades us and evades those for whom we wish good.

All of us, aware of truth, must accept the spiritual responsibility of *being* the god of our individual universes. We can no longer "pass by" without actively *being the truth* of all and for all in our consciousness.

This is the higher meaning of "Love thy neighbor as thyself." Matthew 22:39

The Master gives us an example:

> Who is my neighbour? And Jesus answering said, A certain man went down from Jerusalem to Jericho, and fell among thieves, which stripped him of his raiment, and wounded him, and

departed, leaving him half dead.

And by chance there came down a certain priest that way: and when he saw him, he passed by on the other side. And likewise a Levite, when he was at the place, came and looked on him, and passed by on the other side.

But a certain Samaritan, as he journeyed, came where he was: and when he saw him, he had compassion on him, and went to him, and bound up his wounds, pouring in oil and wine, and set him on his own beast, and brought him to an inn, and took care of him.

And on the morrow when he departed, he took out two pence, and gave them to the host, and said unto him, Take care of him; and whatsoever thou spendest more, when I come again, I will repay thee.

Which now of these three, thinkest thou, was neighbour unto him that fell among the thieves? And he said, He that shewed mercy on him. Then said Jesus unto him, Go, and do thou likewise. Luke 10: 29-37

LESSON
FIFTY-FIVE

You have the innate power — you *are* the innate power, you *are* the innate consciousness — to heal every person who comes into your awareness.

You have the power to reveal the harmony of every thing and condition that comes into your awareness.

You are and have the infinite power of good.

You have the power, you are the power, that finds no resistance to itself anywhere in the world or universe — *not as a personal self with personal power,* but as *(only and exclusively as)* a state of God consciousness.

In God consciousness, you are the presence of God *as,* and *to,* and *for* every person, thing and condition; you have infinite resource, omnipresent and unconditional resource of every good.

We must take up the spiritual responsibility of being the god of our universes. We must be actively god; we must be alive, vital as God consciousness as earth; we must be "thy will be done on earth as it is in heaven."

The God truth of you, of me, of every spiritually aware individual is literal and perfectly demonstrable. We must now *accept it* as being literal and demonstrable, and get on with "the Father's business" of *being* the light of the world, never again content to "pass by."

LESSON
FIFTY-SIX

You have the power of life — the one almighty, all-present, unconditional, non-resistive power of life throughout your world and universe.

You have the power to bring the fullness of life to every single person who walks into your consciousness.

That power, which constitutes its own evidence, which *is* its own evidence, is *God consciousness* (but remember what that means, as clarified throughout these pages).

From the moment we know this truth, we must accept and adopt the spiritual responsibility of *being it.*

Let us accept that responsibility from this moment on. Let us constantly be about the Father's business.

Let us never again pass by without actively knowing and being the truth of all, of limitlessly giving to and serving all in every way.

LESSON
FIFTY-SEVEN

Not one individual with the consciousness of the power of universal life could hold it in, hold it back; could keep from constantly, freely giving it and serving it to the world.

Not one of us, from the minute we have sufficiently awakened to the fact that we are and have the one almighty power of life, could pass by even one of our brothers and sisters without freely giving the gift of true and immediately evident life.

How could we possess an infinity of the greatest gifts of heaven and earth (which each and every one of us does), *knowing* that they are ours to give, yet not be about the business of giving them?

"I must be [it is my responsibility to be] about my Father's business."

LESSON
FIFTY-EIGHT

You are and have the *power of* harmony and peace, and the *power to witness* harmony and peace, here and now, as *all* in your consciousness.

We cannot "pass by" from the minute we know this truth.

We cannot ignore the truth we know by keeping it locked inside a personal or even selfish sense of self, or under the guise of not yet knowing truth "sufficiently." Only a personal sense of self can believe in "insufficient" truth. The minute God-self is realized by even one degree, then of course all God power, presence, form and visibility is known to be God's, not "ours," and is, therefore, limitless, omnipresent and unconditional in individual experience *for its giving to and serving of all equally in our worlds.*

LESSON
FIFTY-NINE

Let us hear this clearly, and take heed.

It is only as we have risen to realize what "God consciousness" actually is and means in experience, and only as we then realize our spiritual responsibility and exercise it (constantly be about the Father's business of *being the god* of our worlds) that we finally break free of the parenthesis of human-hood, of "this world," of the entire pairs of opposites; and find ourselves in limitlessness, in the mind, body and universe of love, grace; in the heavenly state of existence in which all is God.

We cannot break free of the "parenthesis in eternity" until *we ourselves are being the freedom of it.*

We cannot break free of it while we are still in it, while we still believe it and involve ourselves in battles with it, trying to avoid it or heal it, trying to gain its good and be rid of its bad.

If we are "battling" (attempting to avoid or pacify or heal or harmonize or free ourselves of) disease or injury, lack or limitation, discord or unhappiness *at its own level,* we are still firmly in and of the parenthesis in eternity — the pairs of opposites, "this world"; and we cannot get out. We've unwittingly imprisoned ourselves and thrown out the key.

Luckily, the key that locked us in is not the same key that gets us out.

Do not look for the truth key, the key that frees you (heals, prospers, harmonizes you) among humanity, in or for the mental mind, in or for the physical body, in or for the material world. "Not by might, nor by power, but by my spirit, says the Lord of hosts [says the truth of objectivity, the truth of experience]."

We cannot break free of the eternal round of humanity unless and until we are being the freedom of it and for it. In other words, it is only as we take up our spiritual responsibility and be the god of our worlds that we discover ourselves free of falsity and limit, and in the place gods exist, the heavenly place, the Garden of Eden, paradise.

We must *be it* to experience it; *be* freedom to experience freedom; *be a god as and for all* to experience God as all.

LESSON
SIXTY

How can we be busy getting on with the Father's business when we are already busy with family, friends, work or business, and other commitments in our lives?

The miracle of truth is this. God is all, already and forever finished and perfect being, mind, body, form, condition, activity, place, amount.

Because God is all, and because *God itself constitutes* all the good that good is — all the visible, tangible, here and now good of all in our consciousness — all we have to do is *seek God itself;* all we have to do is commune with God; all we have to do is stay attentive to, stay abiding in, God to *witness* God, good, fulfillment — health, love, abundance; food, clothing, home, safety — as and for all in our consciousness.

God — God consciousness, God presence happening as us (as we abide in God and God in us) — *constitutes* all visible fulfillment of our objective experience, of our world.

Again, God, God consciousness, *constitutes* all here-now, visible good form -- good person, good mind, healthy, vital, youthful body; fed, clothed, housed individuals, families, multitudes; our harmonious, peaceful, fulfilled world.

Therefore, the miracle of being about the Father's business is that all we have to do is *stay in God* (not slip out into humanity, physicality or materiality; not be interested in or attentive to the human, physical or material, to thing and condition, to that which seems to be); be interested in and attentive to God itself to *see* and to *have* the visible and tangible form of "all the rest."

Our one-pointed God consciousness opens our eyes to the infinite variety of truthfully sensed allness.

In other words, one with God is a majority.

One with God is *the* majority.

One with God reveals the good that all actually is.

LESSON
SIXTY-ONE

Being one with God does not mean that there is a "you" filled with the awareness of "God". It means *God consciously being the existence you are in the absence of "you"*.

It means that we know that *God is conscious here*, not "we ourselves"; and that we *yield to God being conscious as "our" consciousness*.

"I live, yet not I, Christ lives in me [as the sun lives in the sunbeam]."

The sun lives as its universal self; the sun is *able* to live as its universal self because the sunbeam offers no resistance — has no thoughts of its own, does not have an opinion, a perception of what "is" or what is "not"; does not judge, does not attempt to create or maintain its own life, happiness, success; does not attempt to earn or even evidence its own supply for its own endeavor; does not have its own body, family, friend, student, house, town, country, world.

"I live, yet not I. . . ." Not one single breath or cell or aspect of the awareness of "I" is "mine". *Only God is.*

The Miracle Self has given us the same truth stated as, *Where you are absent, God is present.*

Only God is. Oh, if only the students of the world would truly, deeply, consistently meditate with this one statement (this statement of oneness), freedom and the treasures of heaven and earth (heaven as earth) would so quickly be theirs!

Only God is. Think, think!

What do you think of when you think "I, me, mine"; when you observe a person, an object, a place; when an amount or a condition presents itself to you; when a sound or fragrance fills your senses; when a suggestion of a good or bad person or circumstance presents itself to you?

If there is still a smidgen of God "and" living in us — still a belief in "person, thing or condition" as being entities, realities, separate and different from God instead of the very full and complete presence of God — then the personal self is still living in us, not God.

God consciousness *is, sees* and *has* only *itself* — God appearing to be, through objective sense, "person, thing and condition." But there is no actual "person, thing and condition" separate from each other and God, different from each other and God, isolated entities in and among the infinite.

Only God is.

And because God is *omnipresent* (better stated, God is omnipre*sence,* so that any and every presence is known and accepted as omnipresent God) all is the all-ness of God — good, love, joy, wholeness, fulfillment.

"I am come that ye might have life, and that ye might have it more abundantly." John 10:10

> Hitherto have ye asked [been aware of, sought] nothing in my name [in true God consciousness, in oneness consciousness, in omnipresence consciousness]: ask, and ye shall receive, that your joy may be full. . . . that they might have my joy fulfilled in themselves. John 16:24; 17:13

LESSON
SIXTY-TWO

Today, and of course, eternally, live with the vital awareness of *God being conscious here,* not "you"; that *everything you are conscious of is God* — not "in potential," not "ultimately," not "in reality," not buried deep "within," not "ethereally" or "spiritually" or "in truth," but *is . . . is . . . is.*

God *is;* God *is* the *only is.* If anything whatsoever *is,* it is God. There is nothing "inner" or "outer," as thought or as form, as sight, hearing, taste, touch or smell that is not God. *Only God is.*

"I live, yet not I, Christ lives in me . . . I do not frustrate the grace of God: for if righteousness comes by means of the law, then [Jesus the] Christ died in vain." Galatians 2:20-21

I do not [I will make sure I do not] frustrate the grace of God by dividing my awareness, by accepting *anything* I am

conscious of as being different and separate from God; as
being God "within" or "in truth" or "in reality" but not
"without," not palpably here and now, not "inside and
outside; in short, not *all-of-all* without exception."

> for if [it is believed that] righteousness [the glory,
> clarity, one reality, visibility of truth] comes by
> means of the law [by means of humanity, mind,
> body, matter], then [Jesus the] Christ died in vain
> [the message of truth, of God-being-*all*, has not
> been heard; and the ceaseless, selfless devotion,
> demonstration and teaching of the Master has
> been in vain].

Take *only-God-is* ever — hourly — more deeply into
meditation to the point of realization.

Only *realized* truth is *evident* truth.

Realization *is* evidence, *is* visibility, *is* reality revealed.

LESSON
SIXTY-THREE

Thy word is true from the beginning [is the one true essence, principle, presence and form of all]: and every one of thy righteous judgments [true God awareness or consciousness; true image and likeness of God as all; God cause being God effect] endures for ever. Psalm 119:160

Only God is.

God is infinite; therefore God is the only being, mind, body, thing and condition.

Think deeply about this. God is *infinite;* therefore nothing, nothing, *nothing* "else" exists.

Isn't it fascinating how the intellect accepts this, yet, in parallel, accepts "another"? How can God be *infinite,* yet there also be another? It cannot be. God is infinite; God is *the infinite;* infinity *is God.* God is *the only . . .* the *only, only, only!*

And God is *one;* therefore there is only one law, and it is not only self-operative, but *is itself* the only formation, the only presence, the only substance, the only activity, the only consciousness.

There are no other laws. "Otherness," in the infinity of *one,* is nonsensical to believe and entertain.

Only God is law; only oneness is law; only good is law.

Wash all "otherness" out of you by deeply and consistently pondering God as infinity, God as one, God as the one law, there being no other law operating anywhere at any time under any circumstance whatsoever.

How could the infinity of one be subject to location, time or circumstance? There aren't any. Only God is, only one is, only one law is.

One

One law

One law of mind

One law of body

One law of world

One law of thing, condition, place, amount.

Do not attempt to *relate* the one law *to* any person, thing or condition — to anything you can define. If we attempt that, what have we just done? Stepped out of oneness, therefore out of the one law. We've left ourselves bare and exposed to the chaos of every believed law, and now we're in trouble. The only way to deal with or try to manage the chaos of believed law (the countless laws of opposites; of both good and bad mind, body and world) is by using the laws of believed good to overcome or correct or heal the laws of believed bad; to replace one belief with another, better belief.

Has all this anything to do with God? No. The actual presence and experience of God is nowhere to found in us as long as we are out of conscious oneness and continue looking to and reaching for outer help from person, pill or procedure, from effort or opportunity.

Forever stay in *oneness*, in conscious awareness of the *one law*, one God; one self-sustained finished kingdom ("My kingdom"); one self-operative, self-complete, self-formed, self-alive, self-visible, self-fulfilled law.

LESSON
SIXTY-FOUR

Only *God is;* only *God is law.*

In God consciousness, the world does not have its own laws.

There is not one single law of this world in itself, good or bad.

There is not one single law of mental mind in itself, good or bad.

There is not one single law of a physical body in itself, good or bad.

There is not one single law of matter, or amount, or condition, or place, or time, or space, or cause, or effect in itself, good or bad.

Only God is.

"The Lord is our judge [our consciousness, our awareness], the Lord is our lawgiver [the one law, one power, one omni-God-active form], the Lord is our king; he will save us." Isaiah 33:22

If only God is, what is the only thing to think about? What is the only thing to be aware of? What is the only visibility, the only palpability, the only reality, the only form? Who is the only person? What is the only mind? What is the only body? What is the only cause? God.

If God is the only cause, God is the only *effect.* Therefore, we have nothing to meet, nothing to take thought for, nothing to desire, nothing to suffer, nothing to correct or heal. If it seems as if we do, or are, it is false, with no law to sustain it in our experience *as long as we are not being the believed law of it.*

The minute we *truly turn to God and stay there,* all falsity evaporates because it isn't an entity with a law to sustain it. It is nothing — nothing but accepted belief, which quickly evaporates in the presence of God (in God consciousness, *oneness* consciousness).

LESSON
SIXTY-FIVE

Only God is.

But you see, "If you wish to worship God, you must worship him *in spirit and in truth*." This is the same statement as our *only God is*. Well, if only God is we must recognize and rely on *God itself as itself, as all of all.*

By recognizing, and living with *only God is*, and in knowing that God is spirit and truth, we *are* worshiping God, loving God, devoted to God instead of accepting humanity and this world as it seems to be.

"If I bear witness of myself, my witness is not true."

John 5:31

If we bear witness to a human being, a thing, a condition, our witness is not true and, therefore, cannot "react" to us, cannot *reveal itself* as its true image and likeness.

Everything in My Universe is "shy," or "jealous." We have to be faithful.

We have to love God with everything we are and have, with every sense at every moment.

"God is a jealous God." Exodus 34:14

"Hitherto have you asked nothing in my name: ask, and ye shall receive, that your joy may be full." John 16:24

LESSON
SIXTY-SIX

Only God is; the *name* of God is the *only name.*

If you saw me walking along the street, and you called out "Peter" or "Simon" or "Mary," I would not react. I *could* not react, because your calling out a name that isn't mine has no reaction in me. Nothing stirs in me. I do not hear it.

But the second you call out "Paul," I hear, I react. I *can* now react. You have called in my name.

The same is true of My Universe, My Kingdom, and all it constitutes.

All is God, *only* God is.

Unless we call in *its name,* it doesn't hear us. It cannot react. We are strangers to it. It can only react as we are its friend, its lover, when we know and call out its true name.

In Scripture we hear it stated as "a jealous God."

"I the Lord thy God am a jealous God. . . . thou shalt worship no other god: for the Lord, whose name is Jealous, is a jealous God: lest thou make a covenant with the inhabitants of the land, and they go a whoring after their gods, and do sacrifice unto their gods. . . . Joshua said unto the people, Ye cannot serve [use] the Lord: for he is an holy God; he is a jealous God [all principle is "jealous"; principle can never be used for non-principled effect; principle can only be adhered to]; he will not forgive your transgressions nor your sins [your unwitting non-God, belief, divided consciousness existence]." Exodus 25:5; 34:14-15; Joshua 24:19

The Master takes pains to explain the secret of oneness to us. Six times in the Gospel of John alone, he gives it to us:

"Whatsoever ye shall ask in my name, that will I do, that the Father may be glorified in the Son." John 14:13

"If ye shall ask any thing in my name, I will do it." John 14:14

"The Comforter, which is the Holy Ghost, whom the Father will send [will reveal] in my name [when my name is sought], he shall teach you all things, and bring all things to your remembrance, whatsoever I have said unto you [in other words, every promise of truth]." John 14:26

"Ye have not chosen me, but I have chosen you, and ordained you, that ye should go and bring forth fruit, and that your fruit should remain: that whatsoever ye shall ask of the Father in my name, he will give it you." John 15:16

"And in that day ye shall ask me nothing [in the day of your true realization that all is God, you no longer need instruction or further understanding; you no longer need truth books or classes]. Verily, verily, I say unto you, Whatsoever ye shall ask the Father in my name, he will give it you. [From this point onward, you go straight to the Father, rather than through teacher, class or book]." John 16:23

"Hitherto have ye asked nothing in my name: ask, and ye shall receive, that your joy may be full." John 16:24

LESSON SIXTY-SEVEN

Only God is.
　　Only God is law.
　　Our work from this day onward is to literally live in the consciousness of, and to one hundred percent rely on, *God itself alone as being the one reality of fully manifested, demonstrated, visible, tangible good.*

　　This is what I ask you to hear, and to live by, from this day. The whole of existence — all that God, good, is and has, and all the ways of good; the one law of good, the one form and visibility of good — exists within, and as, your consciousness.

　　It is time to take this truth literally. But let us understand what this means.

We will no longer look for *anything* of God, anything of good, whatsoever, from *outside* of us.

We will no longer look for or to person, pill, procedure, amount, opportunity, place, condition, activity.

We will no longer use the mind to concoct ideas of good, and how to get them.

We will no longer think in terms of, or desire, any object of good, amount of sufficiency, person of love, family of harmony, activity of gain, place of fulfillment.

We will no longer think or act in terms of "mine" versus "another's."

We will no longer believe in and attempt to get or gain anything whatsoever, in itself, from the outer, from the world, from professional or expert, from friend or contact.

We will no longer attempt to "use" our advantage in the world, or our strength or reputation.

We will not even reach for a simple pill to relieve our pain believing that it of itself has power to pacify or heal, that it of itself is a "good law" able to nullify a "bad law."

Live by God alone as the one, literal, real existence — the real existence that is more real, palpable, visible, accessible and effective than any physical or material "reality."

God — the one literal, fully demonstrated, manifested, visible reality — is "closer than breathing, nearer than hands and feet."

This being literally true, why take a breath before having our visible, tangible good?

We are and have all good — infinite, unconditional good — now.

Why move a hand or a foot before having our good?

We are and have all good — infinite, unconditional good — now.

"Not by might, nor by power, but by my spirit, says the Lord of hosts."

LESSON
SIXTY-EIGHT

Only God is, and God is silence.
   Only silence is.
   Only silence is God evident, law evident, true image and likeness evident.

It must be realized that only in our utter silence, our absence of self, our giving of our whole being and its universe over to God, is God visible and real (to our sense) *as* self and universe.

Only God is; therefore only God *can.*

Each day, we must devote time (3, 4 hours minimum) to letting God *be* what *only God is* as us and our universe.

Only God itself is visible as God itself, as all. God is its own evidence.

Nothing, nothing but God itself is evident God, good

— nothing, nothing, nothing.

"Not by might, nor by power, but by my spirit says the Lord of hosts. Zechariah 4:6

"It is the spirit that quickens; the flesh profits nothing." John 6:63

"The entrance of thy words gives light; it gives understanding unto the simple." Psalm 119:130

It is only as we devote ourselves to sitting with God, listening to God, being open and receptive to God, giving our whole beings to God as God for God, that we experience the true universe . . . that being full of good, oneness and omnipresence.

LESSON
SIXTY-NINE

"I have food to eat that ye know not of." It is right here in my lap — an infinity of the best, freshest, most delicious, most satisfying food, that I've had to take no thought for whatsoever.

But if you're looking materially you cannot see it, nor can you eat of it; nor can you feed anyone else with it, which is the worst aspect of material sense.

If we ourselves have insufficient food today, we can probably suffer it to be so. But if our brothers and sisters have to starve because of our inability to feed them with the true, everlasting food, shame on us who are experienced in truth, yet lacking the one discipline and devotion to *let God be the life and presence of us* for a sufficient number of hours every day, which *is itself* the food, is itself the life, is itself the light and form and visibility of every freedom and fulfillment.

Silence is not being about our business while keeping our minds on God.

Silence is not even being about our business while feeling the *presence* of God.

These are good, true and necessary. But the only state in which God is visible and tangible to sense is when *God itself is being* the visibility and tangibility "for us"; when "we" have emptied ourselves out and given ourselves over to that which we truly are: God; when we become the puppet and let God be the puppeteer; when we of our own selves are nothing (when we have stopped, for this hour, trying to *be* something, *know* something, and witness something that we're hoping will evidence God. It will not; it cannot), and we let God be everything.

LESSON SEVENTY

Let God be everything.

If God is everything (which God is) and we are consciously, actively letting God be everything we are and have, what else is there for *us* to be, or to evidence? What else is there for us to do for another?

Oh, our branches fill with the best fruits as we let God be everything; and we *give of* and *serve with* those fruits, abundantly — abundantly. But "we" are out of the equation as any kind of cause or effect, as any kind of personal entity or achiever.

God is all; we of our selves are nothing. So let God be all as and "through" your silence.

LESSON
SEVENTY-ONE

Silence . . . just sitting with God, listening to everything God is and has, like sitting on a mountain top with God, or sitting, "God and I," on the beach or in the forest, listening to the wonders, the miracles, the wisdoms, the *love* that God is and has as us, listening to and being shown the treasures of heaven, the pathways of Paradise — this is the miracle of life.

Then we discover that that miracle turns up here, there and everywhere, inside and outside, *looking like* everything we can describe as being very good throughout our universe; all the life, all the love, all the food, all the home, all the clothes, all the safety and security, all the happiness of being, and fulfillment of purpose — not only for "us" (there is not very much of "us" left, even though "we," like the branch of the vine, find ourselves filled with fruit), but of all and for all our brothers and sisters who touch our consciousness.

"To this end was I born, and for this cause came I into the world, that I should bear witness unto the truth. Every one that is of the truth hears my voice." John 18:37

Let us, each and every one, fulfill our cause, our reason for being, and devote the rest of time to bearing witness unto the truth.

In this way and this way alone, are we the freedom of spirit, therefore the freedom from the eternal round of human parenthesis.

Finally, we are free in God as a god, and therefore are the freedom of all in our universe.

My Universe has been attained; My Kingdom is now visible, real, tangible; and all is very good, very purposeful, very God.

90766120R00093

Made in the USA
Columbia, SC
09 March 2018